CW00868091

Squash Basics: How to Play Squash

ISBN-13: 978-1475229516

ISBN-10: 1475229518

SQUASH BASICS: HOW TO PLAY SQUASH

Maria Gheeny

I dedicate this book to every person – who has been lucky enough to have their lives touched by the joy, excitement and sheer buzz of squash...

Contents

Why Play Squash?

Most people don't understand the game of squash, but those who've played racquetball at some point may have watched other people use the same court for squash.

In fact, this sport pre-dates racquetball by hundreds of years and is played by many people from all over the world. It was originally played by hitting the ball with the palm of your hand.

That practice only stopped when squash racquets were invented and these days, racquets for this sport is made of the most high-tech materials your money can buy.

Another major change is that the sport is now played at break-neck speed. In order to become a good squash player, therefore, you'll need a great deal of talent, skill, agility, and a quick mind.

These attributes are needed for tracking the ball and getting to it in time as well as for predicting the ball's next location and avoid getting hit by it.

Whoever reaches nine points first wins in this fast-paced game.

And while using the side walls is a normal part of the game, there are specific rules you need to follow.

Bear in mind that squash isn't a sport for wimps, especially since injuries are fairly common among serious players. It can be the ideal sport for people who love competition and are in good physical shape.

People who are no longer in their prime should play only with similarly-skilled players in order to enjoy the sport and avoid injury.

Because of constant efforts from squash enthusiasts, the sport is now sanctioned by the Olympics. When watching squash games at the Olympics, you get to see deadly-accurate players flying across the court at seemingly impossible angles in efforts to return the ball to the front wall.

A large part of the enjoyment of watching a game of squash has to do with the fact that it is one of the few sports that aren't dominated by US teams, which gives it so much more variety and makes it so much more competitive where global tournaments are concerned.

Squash isn't just exciting to play, but to watch as well.

Squash is indeed a true test of a person's agility, as anyone playing in any of the 50,000 courts around the world can attest.

And perhaps the only reason you haven't noticed the beauty of the game is that you haven't really been watching it.

After reading this book, though, you may be prepared to expand your horizons and start taking a closer look at the game of squash.

Who knows, you may soon join the ranks of squash fans. And if you think you're physically and mentally up for it, you may even want to try a game or two.

No matter how good you think your physical condition is, you'll surely find squash very challenging and a 30-minute game is sure to get you feeling sore and tired in a way you've never been in your entire life.

Despite the soreness, though, the fun and excitement will surely have you looking forward to your next game.

What to Look For in a Racquet

When you decide to start playing squash, you'd naturally need to find a good squash racquet and there are several factors you need to consider when choosing this particular item in your squash arsenal.

Squash racquets have several different features you should take note of when you choose which one to buy.

Regardless of your skill level, it's important to have the right racquet not only because it helps improve your play, but also because it complements your methods as a player.

Knowing the characteristics of a particular racquet design can help you find the racquet that's perfect for you.

The first characteristic you need to check is the racquet's weight. A slight difference in weight can have a significant effect in your game, which is why it's an important factor in choosing your racquet.

Racquets of different weights also have different advantages.

A lighter squash racquet is, of course, much easier to handle and will require significantly less strain when you move to hit the ball.

However, a heavier squash racquet provides significantly more power as well as increased momentum when you swing. Heavier racquets therefore help beginners round out their games easily.

Another important characteristic you should check is the racquet's balance. This characteristic depends largely on the weight of the racquet's head, which is generally classified as light, heavy, or neutral.

A racquet with a heavy weight generally has heavy balance as well. In the same way, lighter racquets will have lighter balance and may generally seem like it provides very little power.

Your racquet's stiffness is another characteristic you need to look out for, since it largely dictates power and accuracy.

A stiff racquet will be much more accurate and powerful, but you can only take full advantage of this characteristic once you've developed a good grip and increased squash technique.

The shape of your racquet is another important consideration.

In fact, it's one of the most crucial elements of a squash racquet's design. If your racquet has a larger head surface, it'll allow you to take more powerful shots and it'll increase your consistency as well because the larger head surface makes it a lot easier to hit shots, thus reducing the amount of faulty shots or missed hits.

Another feature to look out for when shopping for a squash racquet is its durability. Remember that squash racquets regularly take a beating throughout an entire game and a well-built racquet made from highly durable materials will ensure that you won't have to keep replacing your racquet.

By choosing a racquet that suits your style of play, you can quickly improve your game.

The good news is that squash racquets come in many designs and styles, so you're sure to find one that perfectly suits your style of play and level of skill.

Always remember that choosing the right racquet can do much to provide you with increased technique and a much better game.

Buying the Right Shoes

In a fast-paced and gruelling game like squash, where rallies often go for long periods of time, you can't afford to play with the wrong kind of equipment or one with inferior quality.

You'll have to be constantly on your toes, as it can be very difficult to kill the ball.

And while most people would naturally think about getting the right racquet first, having the right pair of shoes can actually be more important.

Take note that standard squash etiquette and the rules of many squash courts require you to wear clean shoes that won't leave marks on or cause any damage to the court.

This generally means you can't wear black-soled shoes for a squash game. The reason for this requirement is that dirty shoes or the wrong type of shoes can make the surface uneven or slippery, which often leads to injuries.

Needless to say, the shoes you wear while going to the squash court can't be the same shoes you wear when you play.

Remember as well that there are squash shoes specifically-designed for indoor courts.

These shoes have outer soles that are made of gum rubber, which is very soft and usually blonde or light brown in colour.

Despite their softness, however, these soles are still firm enough to provide the necessary traction for the game.

Take note that the intensity of the game will cause increased blood flow, which in turn, causes your feet to swell a bit during a match.

Considering this, it's advisable to walk around for a minimum of 15 minutes before you go shopping for squash shoes.

This way, your feet are already swollen when you start trying on some shoes.

And once you have a pair of shoes on, try to move around the way you would during a game so you can make sure the shoes are comfortable.

Try to determine if the shoes are stable enough, if your feet aren't slipping around in the shoes, if you can move each foot a bit from heel to toe, if your feet can move around in the foot bed, and if the shoes are long enough such that your toes don't touch the end of the toe box.

Of course, you should make sure the shoes aren't too tight.

You'll know it's time to replace your squash shoes if the soles already look particularly worn or if your feet hurt much more than usual the day after a match.

The way your feet naturally move largely affects how often you need to replace your squash shoes.

For example, if your heel or toes drag, then your shoes may get worn out unevenly and you may have to replace them a lot more often.

In general, squash players replace their shoes as often as they play each week.

For example, if you play four times each week, then you're likely to buy new shoes four times in one season.

Your shoes are among the most important items in your squash arsenal, which is why it's important to make sure you have the right pair.

Buying Goggles

Squash goggles are used to protect your eyes during any game of squash.

Take note that players at the top of their game can hit the squash ball at speeds of up to 125mph; that's something you definitely need to protect your eyes from, considering the fact that it has the possibility of inflicting very serious damage.

The good news is that squash goggles are specifically-designed to keep your eyes safe during a game and they come in a variety of great designs you can choose from.

Of course, there are a few things you should take into consideration when you shop for a pair of squash goggles.

As mentioned above, there are several designs for squash goggles. Some of them are tied around the back of your head for a secure fit, while others are simply held in place like a pair of reading glasses or sunshades.

Remember that if you're already wearing prescription glasses, then you may need to have squash goggles custom-made to address your vision needs.

It's essential to choose a pair of squash goggles that don't impair your peripheral vision, so you're sure to get a good view of the entire court.

This is especially important because any blind spot on a squash court counteracts the entire concept of safety.

It's understandable, of course, for you to look for a pair of goggles with an attractive style or design. But, safety should always be your topmost concern, since it is the most crucial element of squash goggles.

When shopping for a pair of squash goggles, check to make sure that the lenses are shatterproof and that they have anti-fogging properties.

If you find a pair you like, which doesn't have anti-fogging properties, you may apply an anti-fog spray on it, which is readily available at reasonable prices.

What's more important is for the lenses to be shatterproof. You should also make sure the goggles fit comfortably on your head.

These goggles come in junior sizes for younger players as well as those with smaller heads.

It's also advantageous to look for squash goggles that have scratch-resistant lenses.

Always remember that squash is a highly physical sport and there will surely be times when your goggles will get bumps and scratches.

Getting a sturdy pair of goggles helps you ensure that you won't have to keep replacing it and that your vision won't be impaired while wearing it.

Squash goggles are among the most essential items in your squash arsenal. The good thing is that they're inexpensive solutions to the need for protection against the risk of possibly serious injury.

The design of squash goggles is generally centred on safety, but still manages to provide you with little innovations such as anti-fog, scratch-resistance, and comfort.

You'd do well to take your time in checking as many different types and designs of squash goggles as possible.

More importantly, make sure you invest in the right pair of goggles to address your safety needs when enjoying the game of squash.

The Importance of Strings

You probably already know it's important to choose the right racquet in order to do well in the sport of squash, but did you know that your squash strings largely affect the performance of your racquet as well?

You read that right; choosing the right racquet isn't all about weight and balance.

It's about the strings as well.

When the characteristics of your squash strings are changed, several aspects of your performance can be improved.

Changing your strings can also help tailor the setup of your racquet to your style of play.

The good news is that there are plenty of different string dynamics and features you can choose from when you shop for the perfect squash strings for your racquet.

Regardless of what style of play you have, you can use squash string tension to your advantage. If you want to deliver more powerful shots, then the perfect string tension for your racquet is a loose one.

If you're already comfortable with the power of your racquet and you simply want to develop more accuracy and control, then it's best to tighten up your racquet strings.

Another feature you need to take note of is the racquet string thickness, which is often called the gauge.

Thinner strings offer more power primarily because it creates a catapult effect, since a thinner diameter allows it to bend inwards and outwards easily.

Thicker strings, on the other hand, offer added control and durability.

If you want increased accuracy, then you should opt for firmer and less palpable squash strings.

Always remember that your squash racquet strings will naturally lose tension the more you use your racquet.

If you prefer tight strings, then you'll probably notice a decrease in your accuracy and control over time.

When you do, check the tension in your racquet strings, as it's probably already loose.

If you chose looser strings to start with, then you'll probably notice a reduction in the power of your shots as the strings in your squash racquet loosen even more.

The good news is that there's an easy way to address these issues.

You simply need to maintain your equipment's quality (and your game as well) by having your strings tightened regularly or by replacing them when the need arises.

If you're a beginner in this sport and you're still trying to master your game, or even if you're already a pro and you simply wish to polish your squash skills, you should always bear in mind that string tension is an important element in maintaining your equipment.

It's generally estimated that string tension is reduced for up to ten percent each time a squash racquet is used, which is why you need to get it checked and tightened regularly.

Choosing the right strings for your squash racquet is indeed one of the most important steps you need to take as you gear up for this sport.

Make sure your strings have the right tension and gauge to complement your style of play.

Furthermore, make sure your equipment is regularly maintained so you can ensure consistency in your game.

What You Need to Know

In the sport of squash, the term "grips" can mean any of two things.

First, it refers to the methods players use in holding their racquet during a game.

Second, it refers to the material used on the end of a squash racquet to help improve a player's grip.

Regardless of what it means, grips are important factors to consider when learning how to play squash.

It's important for you to gain full understanding of how the different ways of holding your squash racquet can affect your performance.

At the same time, it's also important for you to choose good grip material for your racquet.

In general, the method you use in gripping your squash racquet largely depends on your personal preference and the style that works best for you.

There are, however, some quick tips that can help you improve your grip and therefore improve your game.

There are different advantages to holding the grip towards the bottom of your racquet and holding it higher up the racquet.

By holding the low end of your squash grip, you can successfully increase leverage and reach, which will allow you to make shots that would otherwise just zip by you.

On the other hand, holding the grip higher up the racquet gives you more control, making the racquet feel lighter and allowing you to react more quickly for drop shots and quick volleys.

This also allows you to respond to deep back wall shots more successfully.

You should also remember that it's necessary to replace the grip on your squash racquet from time to time in order to keep your grip effective.

Overusing your grips can cause it to become slippery, which can affect your game in a negative way.

The good news is that it's easy enough to replace your racquet grips. What's a bit more difficult is finding the right grip.

There are various kinds of grip material and you'll need a little research to find the one that's perfect for you.

If you're looking for extra bulk to make your racquet grip more comfortable and easier to hold, then a thin over-grip may be your best option. if, however, you're replacing your entire squash racquet grip, then you need to choose a thicker grip.

When choosing a grip tape, you'll need to check features such as tackiness that allows better grip and how dry the grip will be while in use.

Your choice of colours and styles may depend entirely on your personal preference as long as you make sure your grips are of the right type and have the right features.

Developing the ability to hold your squash racquet properly is the key to improving your game.

Choosing grip material of excellent quality will also provide you with much-needed edge in this sport where the racquet is perhaps the most important piece of equipment for ensuring success.

The good thing is that grips are relatively low-priced, which makes it easy enough for you to regularly replace it and ensure the professional upkeep and maintenance of your squash equipment.

How to Play

Besides being a luscious vegetable, squash is a fast-paced racquet sports that dates back to the 16th century.

Generally, the game is played by two opposing players in a four-walled court. Using their respective racquets, the players knock a ball against the wall.

There are also games with four players and just like other racquet sports, these games are known as doubles matches.

Squash aficionados have been lobbying for some time to get the sport included in the Olympic Games.

Squash has gained popularity in many parts of the world primarily because it doesn't need much playing space.

In fact, a significant number of gyms and health clubs now have squash courts.

The court

As mentioned above, a squash court is a four-walled playing area.

It has a horizontal line separating the front from the back area and another line separating the left from the right part of the rear court.

The playing area of the game is therefore divided into three boxes.

The front wall of a squash court is designated as the leading playing floor and has three parallel horizontal stripes.

The topmost line, which is known as the "out line," also runs along the sides in a descending manner.

Aside from the descending out line, the side and back walls have no further markings.

The first player to serve in squash gets to decide whether to serve from the right or left service box. When serving, one of the player's feet has to be inside the service box without making contact with any of the lines.

Once served, the ball should hit the front wall anywhere between the out line and the service line.

After it hits the wall, the ball should then land on the opposite side of the court and then the opposing player decides whether to volley the ball or not.

If the serving player wins the point in a volley, the players will have to exchange sides in preparation for the next serve.

During a squash volley, the opposing players take turns hitting the ball and as long as the ball keeps hitting the front wall below the out line, the ball is kept in play.

The ball may hit the side and back walls at any time while in play, but it can only hit the floor once.

Furthermore, the ball shouldn't hit the floor before hitting the front wall during a serve. The ball can only bounce once on the floor after it has hit the front wall and then the non-serving player has to hit it for the return.

There are no limits as to how many times the ball can hit the side or back wall.

Squash is a fast-paced and typically powerful recreational activity that requires excellent hand-eye coordination.

While the brief description of the court and the basic rules of the game provided above may be a bit confusing to those who aren't familiar with the game, they'll surely make sense as soon as you set foot on a squash court.

And once you start playing, the thrill of competition is sure to take over and you'll start enjoying every minute of the game.

The Length of a
Squash Game

People who aren't quite familiar with the sport often ask how long a squash game typically lasts.

The answer to this question is quite interesting because it necessarily goes hand-in-hand with how you can make sure you're fit enough both physically and mentally to last for an entire game of squash, considering its stringent demands.

There has been a recent shift both in the amateur and professional games to adopt American or Par scoring wherein every point counts regardless of which player serves.

This scoring system significantly shortens total match time, since the score of each player is constantly moving as they each rally towards their goal of 11 points. Should the players reach a 10-10 tie, one will have to advance by two clear points in order to win the match.

International scoring has a player winning a point only if he was the one who served, thus making a match lengthier.

The longest squash match ever played was between a world champion from Pakistan and Egypt's number one player.

The first game of this match lasted for 75 minutes, with the first point being won only after 15 minutes of play.

The match itself lasted for 2 hours and 46 minutes! Towards the end of the match, the players' legs were already cramping and the match itself even led to the retirement of one of the players just a few years later.

Having to go through that match just drained the spirit out of the player and he just wasn't the same after that, which is why he decided on an early retirement.

What's worse is that he also retired early from life itself when he died of a sudden heart attack in 2004 at the age of 49.

In a women's match, the longest ever recorded lasted for an hour and 57 minutes. With a 90-second break between games and a 5-minute warm up period, the total length of the match was 2 hours and 7 minutes. It was played in Toronto between Rhonda Throne and Vicki Hoffman.

Just like the men's longest match, this one also ended in tragedy because it resulted in the loss of the two Australian players' friendship. At the time, Vicki Hoffman was ranked World Number One and Rhonda Throne, who was her teammate and training partner, was ranked Number Two.

When the match in question reversed those rankings, it was more than Hoffman could take and it took years for her to come to grips with that outcome. Sad to say, this is often the case when a status quo is upset and the new order isn't readily accepted.

What's even sadder is that the match affected Rhonda Throne just as negatively as it did Vicki Hoffman. Having achieved her ultimate goal of becoming the world's number one female squash player, Throne lost her competitive edge, perhaps as a result of feeling that she has proven everything there is to prove about her worth as a player.

Soon after that match and right after the 1983 Women's World Squash Championships, she went into retirement.

Again, this scenario is very common in life; people usually set goals and strive towards achieving it, and once they do, it can be very difficult to shake loose and set a higher or a different goal.

These days, amateur matches last for about 35 minutes and professional matches last for about 45 minutes, thus reducing the physical and emotional demands on the players.

What this means, however, is that the shorter rallies will have much higher intensities than before and the slightest lapse in focus and concentration may cost you a point.

What's important is for you to make sure you're physically and mentally tough enough to handle a match, and emotionally tough enough to handle the outcome of the match.

Key Strategies in Squash

If you want to win in a game of squash, then you'll need to learn a few techniques and strategies that are sure to help you achieve your goal.

Here are two of the most effective squash strategies you can use:

The first and perhaps most effective strategy you need to adopt is recognising what kind of opportunities you have or don't have.

To accomplish this, you'll have to look at where your opponent is standing and whether he's balanced or not.

If he looks even slightly off-balance, then that's the perfect time for you to play a forcing or attacking shot.

If your opponent is leaning forward and looks well-balanced, then you should rally and work on forcing your opponent to the back of the squash court by making the ball go right past him.

If you attempt to hit the ball to the back of the court and your opponent cuts it off, that means your opponent hasn't really moved much and you'll probably need to move more and very quickly because your opponent is likely to volley the ball.

The second strategy can best be explained this way: Try to play the ball from the middle of the squash court and then make your opponent play it from any of the four corners.

You should make sure that each shot you execute allows you to quickly recover to the "T" and balance properly before your opponent can hit the ball.

This strategy is based on a very subtle concept that's best described as "covering your rear end."

Remember that in a game of squash, being close to the "T" allows you to hit the ball hard and execute a "top" attack.

When you're just a couple of steps away from the "T" you need to be significantly more circumspect about the shot you're going to take as well as its execution.

Remember that you need that shot to buy you time and allow you to recover. If the shot fails to do that, then you'll need to run faster than you want and you'll definitely end up getting the worse deal of the rally.

Imagine that you're in a game, standing on the "T," and wearing shorts without any underwear.

As you hit the ball from the "T" you don't really have any problem, but when you need to play the ball from a point away from the "T," your shorts just might start to fall!

And as you run hard into the corner to return a shot, your shorts will likely be pooling around your ankles and you'll most probably be seriously mooning the spectators.

If you recognise this possible scenario beforehand, then you'll probably play a slow and defensive shot that'll give you enough time to return to the "T" and pull your shorts back up.

Of course, this is just an example, but you get the picture.

Simply by keeping these two strategies in mind when you play, you can surely start improving your game and you just might get your very first win in the game of squash.

Keep Your Eyes on the Ball

Watching the ball closely during a squash rally is probably the most important thing you'll ever do to improve your performance in the game.

In fact, you should never take your eyes away from the ball during a rally.

If you're apprehensive about watching the ball when it's behind you, take comfort in the fact that you have squash goggles to protect your face and eyes.

It's downright impossible for you to reach your full potential as a squash player if you don't learn how to keep your eyes on the ball.

For one thing, watching the ball closely as it leaves the surface of your opponent's racquet when he's hitting behind you can dramatically increase your skills in a number of ways.

1. You can judge your opponent's shots more successfully

As the ball leaves your opponent's racquet, you get your first idea of where the shot is going.

You gather information on the trajectory, speed, direction, and height of your opponent's shot and then your brain calculates where you need to meet the shot.

In order to track the ball accurately, you need to keep your eye on it at all times.

If you wait until the ball bounces on the front wall, then you've lost about half of the trajectory input you need in order to judge the shot accurately.

2. You'll be better able to anticipate your opponent's shots

You'll only be able to successfully anticipate your opponent's shot if you watch the ball at that split-second when it comes off of your opponent's racquet.
Take note that learning to anticipate whether your opponent is driving, boasting, dropping, or going cross-court already wins you half of the battle.

Research has shown that expert players don't necessarily have better vision than beginners, but they're definitely able to make better use of the cues they get from watching the ball.

The more matches you play, the better your anticipatory skills will be as long as you remember to always keep your eye on the ball.

3. You'll have better rhythm

Developing the ability to watch the ball even when it's behind you is vital for better movement.

It increases your speed in reaching the ball and allows you to move with the appropriate speed instead of overrunning the ball.

In fact, you should be extra careful about overrunning the ball because this is one of the most common mistakes beginners make.

Watching the ball allows you to move more quickly around the squash court even without becoming physically faster.

Remember that rhythm is very important in any sport, since it facilitates all of your movements.

4. You'll play safer and avoiding decisions made against you

Watching the ball also helps you get out of the way of your opponent's racquet swing while he's returning a shot. I

f you don't watch the ball, then not only will your progress be limited, but it may even be dangerous.

By watching the ball, you can easily step out of the way in case you're too close or if you're in the line of fire. Watching the ball also helps you make better tactical decisions when it's your time to make a shot.

Always remember that not watching the ball when your opponent is hitting behind you is that you can easily be guilty of not clearing or not even attempting to clear.

And that can spell the difference between a stroke and a let in the game of squash.

Squash Doubles: Creating a Winning Partnership

When playing doubles in squash, your topmost priority should be protecting and empowering your partner.

Above all, remember that a good partner sticks to the game plan.

Good partners are predictable and consistent, and they provide understanding and emotional support to each other.

Adopting this kind of attitude allows you to successfully sort out what's going on in a particular match and communicate with your partner effectively on the court.

In fact, adopting this attitude may be the main factor that helps you prevail in the game.

Even if you've been playing with the same partner for several years, remember that neither one of you is a mind reader, so you should still let your partner know how you're feeling or what you're thinking.

When you're feeling especially strong, then you can take responsibility for hitting the big shots during crucial points.

If you're feeling a bit defensive, then it's best for you to play safe until you regain your confidence.

At the same time, however, you should take responsibility for yourself and assess your effectiveness on the court honestly.

Having a warped perspective of how you're playing isn't useful to your team. In fact, it can negatively affect your game.

When you join a tournament as part of a squash doubles team, you're likely to be subjected to a gruelling game schedule.

Take note that many players have been dropped from a team even when they didn't miss even a single return in any of their games for the simple reason that they failed to truly play with their partner.

Playing with your partner means being aware of every shot you hit and how it can affect your partner.

If your partner is slowing down, for example, a hard cross-court that fails to get past your opponents may result in catching your partner out of position and your team without any way of covering the next shot.

As a good partner, you should also play such that you enhance your partner's strengths and cover his weaknesses.

Of course, your partner should do the same for you. Furthermore, you should play to expose your opponents' weaknesses and negate their strengths.

If your opponents like to run, then you should strive to keep them towards the back of the court. If they love hitting hard, then you should float the ball over their heads towards the back court.

If you see an immobile or slow player, then you should move him around the court and strive to drag him forward and back.

You should also make sure any message you send your partner, whether verbal or non-verbal, is clear.

This helps you build relaxation and confidence with your partner and allows both of you to do your respective jobs.

Furthermore, developing faith and trust between you and your partner allows you to play confidently and with decisiveness.

Above all, you should always treat your partner the way you expect to be treated.

Support them through difficulties and celebrate victories with them just as you would with a friend.

Have fun

So all in all squash is a fast-paced sport that sneakily addictive and loads of fun.

Get started today and have fun!

Printed in Great Britain
by Amazon.co.uk, Ltd.,
Marston Gate.